THE DAILY LIFE OF FAMILIES IN COLONIAL AMERICA

US HISTORY FOR KIDS GRADE 3

CHILDREN'S HISTORY BOOKS

Speedy Publishing LLC

40 E. Main St. #1156

Newark, DE 19711

www.speedypublishing.com

Copyright 2017

In this book, we're going to talk about the daily life of families in Colonial America. So, let's get right to it!

FARMING IN COLONIAL AMERICA

I n the early years of the American colonies, most people survived by farming. The work was very difficult and the hours were long. Everyone in the family had tasks to do from sunrise to sunset. Eventually, there were farmers who became wealthy landowners and didn't do most of the hard labor themselves. However, at the beginning, this wasn't true and farmers had to work extremely hard throughout every season to ensure that their families were fed.

EARLY MORNING ON THE FARM

As soon as the sun rose, the farmer and his family were out of the house and dealing with the daily chores. Every single minute was important so they wasted very little time with breakfast. The farmer would sit down at the wooden table and have a bowl of porridge with a glass of beer, before heading out for the daily tasks.

A FAMILY OF FARMERS AFTER A LONG DAY OF HARVESTING

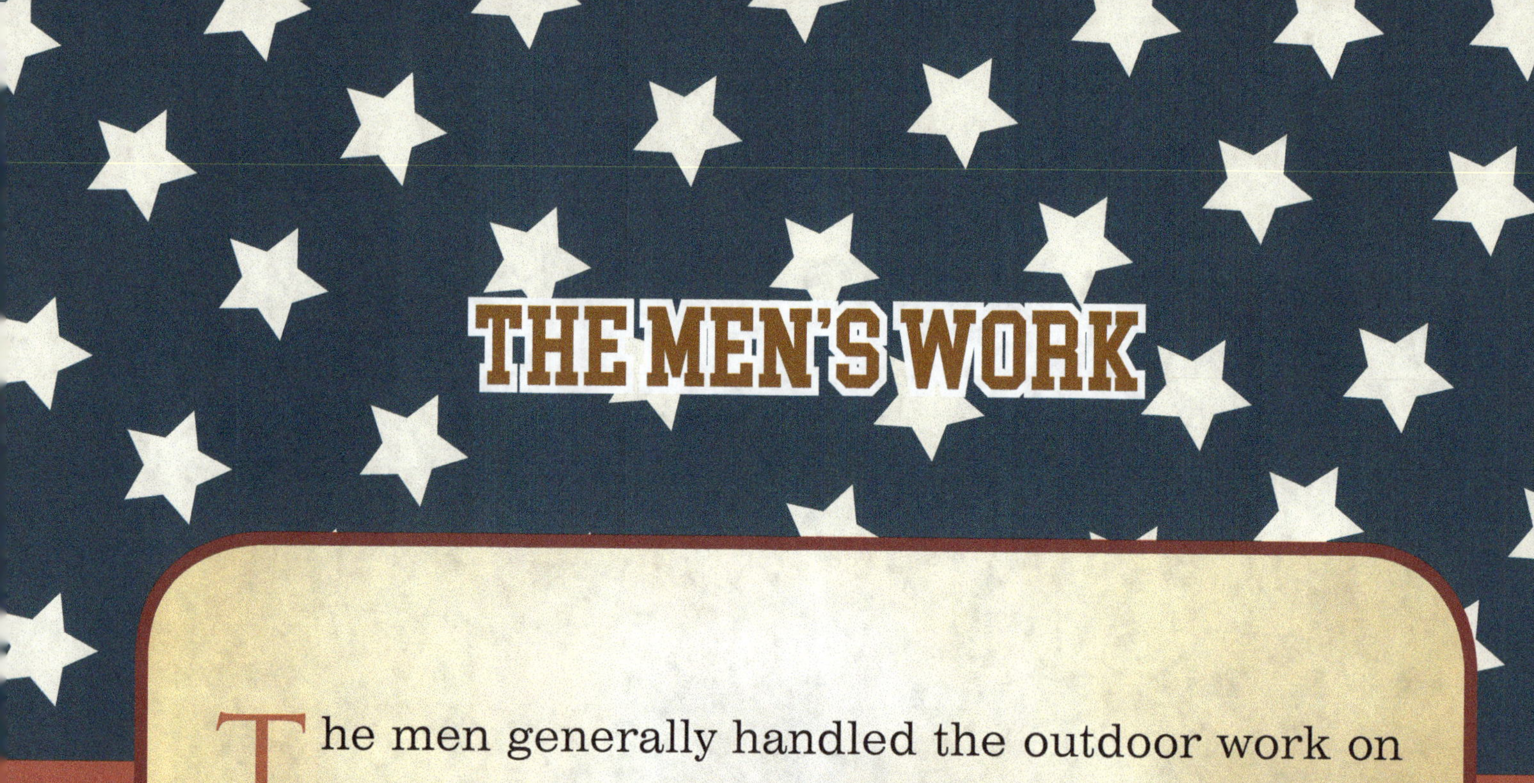

THE MEN'S WORK

The men generally handled the outdoor work on the farm. During the spring, they would till the soil and plant the crops. There were no large machines to help them like on today's farms. They did the work by hand and sometimes had the help of a farm animal like an ox or a horse.

A TYPICAL AMERICAN FARMER

In the fall, it was time for the harvest and they gathered up the crops to sell at the market or store for their own use. During the rest of the year, they maintained the fields, fed the livestock, repaired the farm fences, chopped the firewood, and took care of needed construction around the farmhouse. There was never a lack of work to do.

THE WOMEN'S WORK

The women's work was just as difficult as the men's. Women were in charge of preparing all the meals for the family. They also took care of all the family clothing. They wove the original cloth and stitched as well as mended the clothing.

PREPARING MEALS FOR THE FAMILY

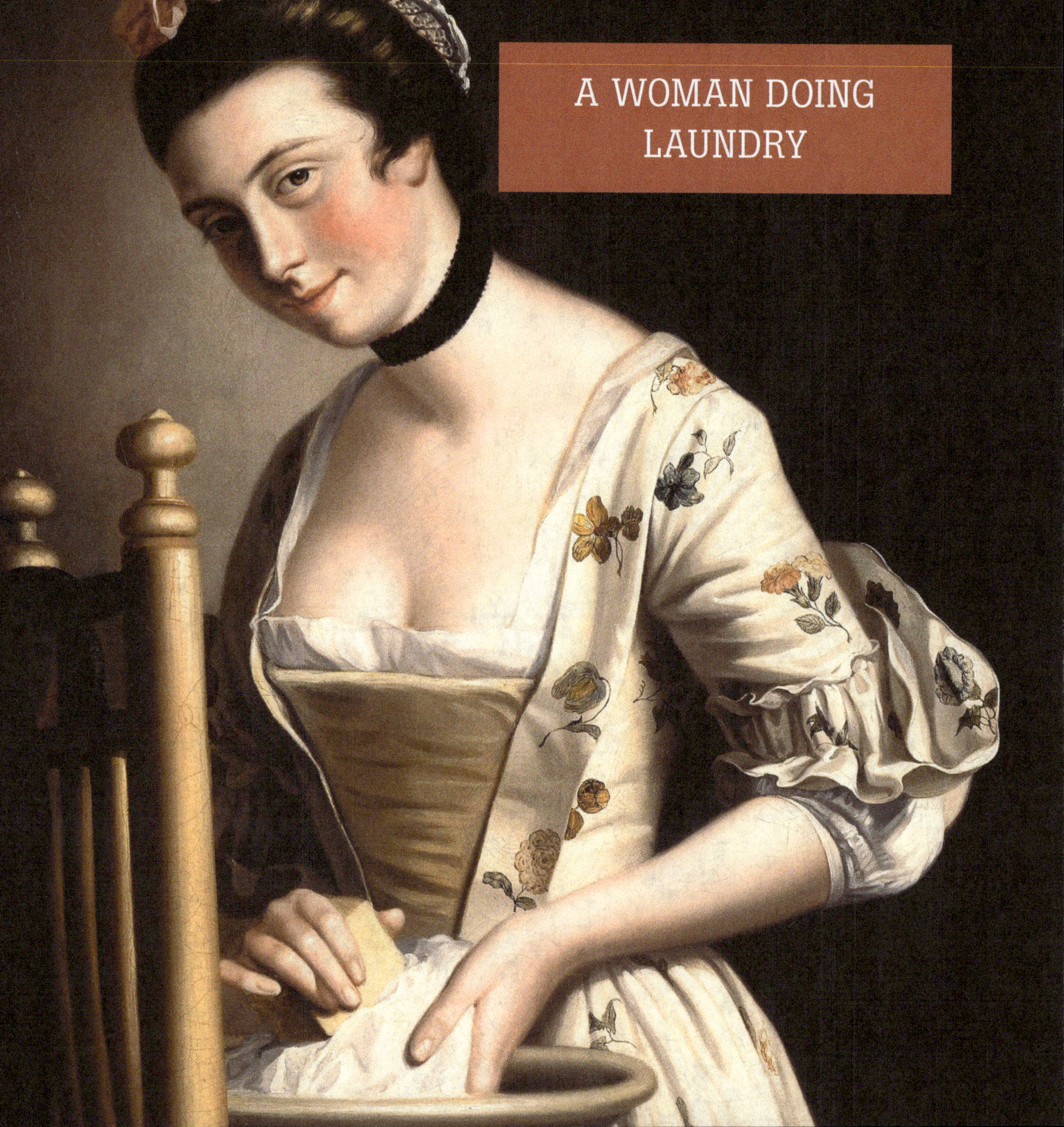
A WOMAN DOING LAUNDRY

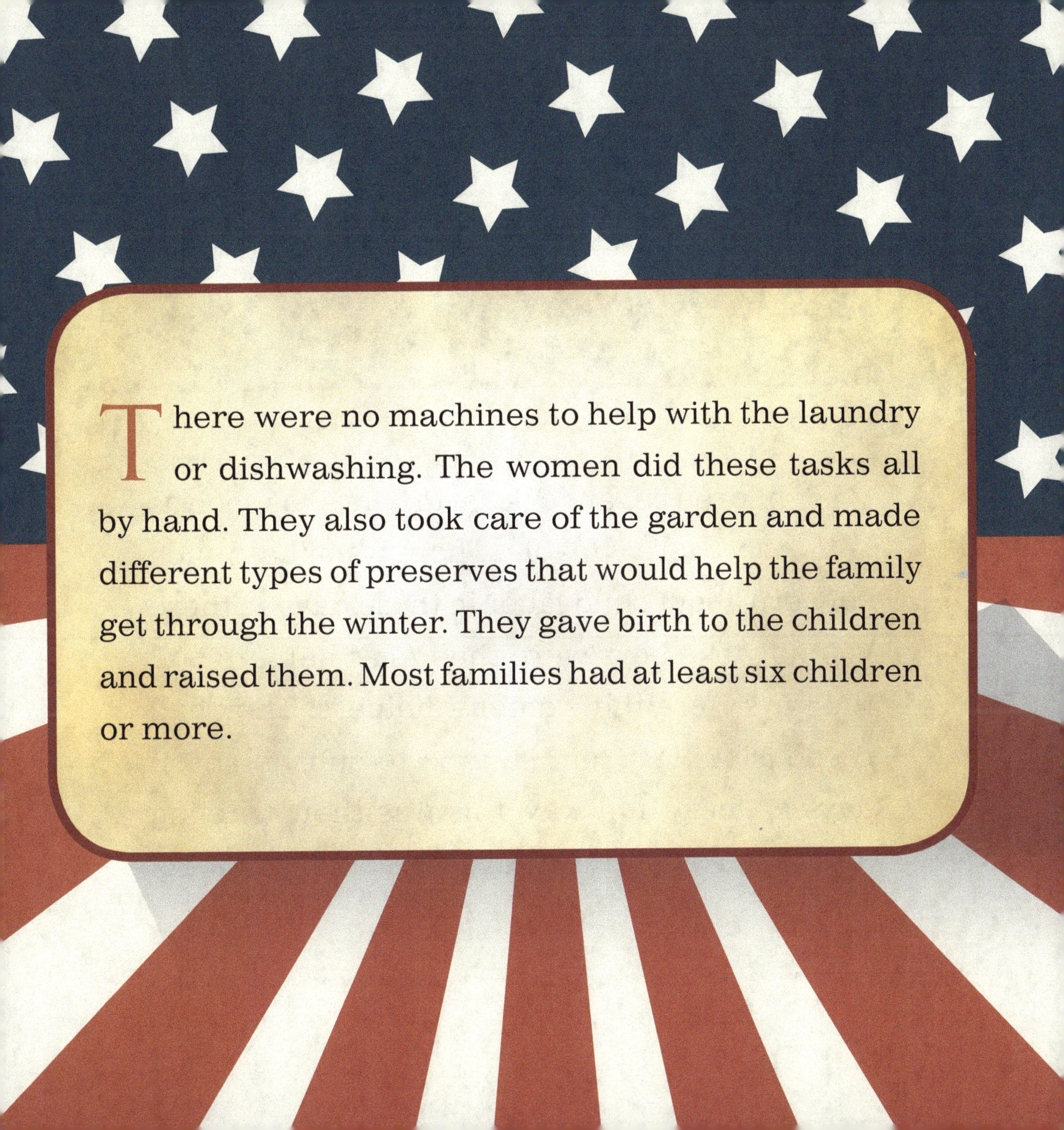

There were no machines to help with the laundry or dishwashing. The women did these tasks all by hand. They also took care of the garden and made different types of preserves that would help the family get through the winter. They gave birth to the children and raised them. Most families had at least six children or more.

THE CHILDREN'S WORK

Children began to do farm chores as soon as they were capable. There wasn't as much concern about child labor in those days as there is today. The boys were the men's helpers and the girls were the women's helpers. They had responsibilities from sunrise to sunset, seven days a week. In a way, this was their training for the life they would have when they grew up.

CULTIVATION OF TOBACCO
AT JAMESTOWN 1615

SUNDAY GATHERING

DID THE CHILDREN GO TO SCHOOL?

In most areas, there weren't any public schools like there are today. Most of the children who lived on farms didn't receive any form of schooling. Sometimes boys were taught how to read and how to write from their fathers or their local ministers who trained them in the Bible's teachings. It wasn't seen as particularly important if girls learned to read or write, so they were not taught those skills as often as boys.

In areas where children did attend school, the boys attended for a longer period of time. It was seen as more important for them to become literate so they could attend to the farm's accounting and business when they got older.

WHAT CROPS DID THEY GROW?

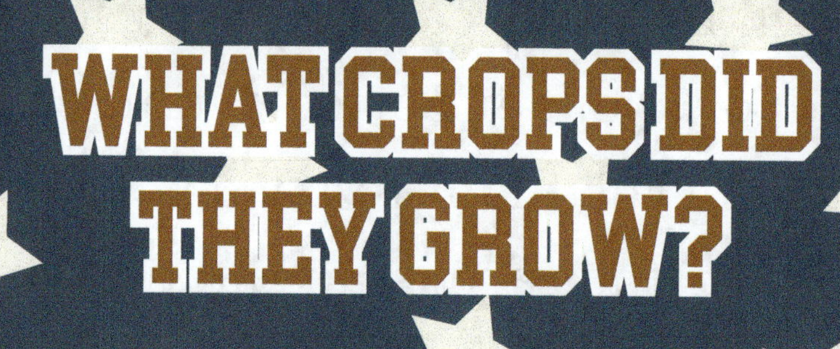

Farmers in the colonies grew many different types of crops depending on the climate of the area they lived. The grains, such as wheat, as well as barley and oats, were common crops. Corn and tobacco were planted frequently as well.

HARVESTING CROPS

DID SLAVES WORK ON THE FARMS?

The first farmers in the colonies didn't own any slaves. However, by the early part of the 1700s there were some wealthy plantation owners who had slaves to work their farms. The everyday farmer couldn't afford to feed a slave in addition to his own family.

DID EVERYONE LIVE ON FARMS?

As more settlers came to the colonies, some towns turned into larger cities. As with any sizable city, there were centers for trade and many types of businesses sprang up. The city family lived very differently than the farming family.

GATHERING IN A TAVERN

People who worked in the cities were craftsmen, artisans, or merchants. There were stores on the main street that offered goods and services for the citizens. There were also restaurants and taverns for eating, drinking, and socializing with neighbors. There was a local blacksmith as well as a pharmacist and a tailor.

WHAT WAS THE MIDDLING CLASS?

The city was where many of the "middling class" people lived. Today we would call them the "middle class." They weren't poor like most of the farming people, but they were also not wealthy like the gentry class was. The middling class consisted of two groups, the tradesmen and the professionals. The professionals were usually more well off than the tradesmen.

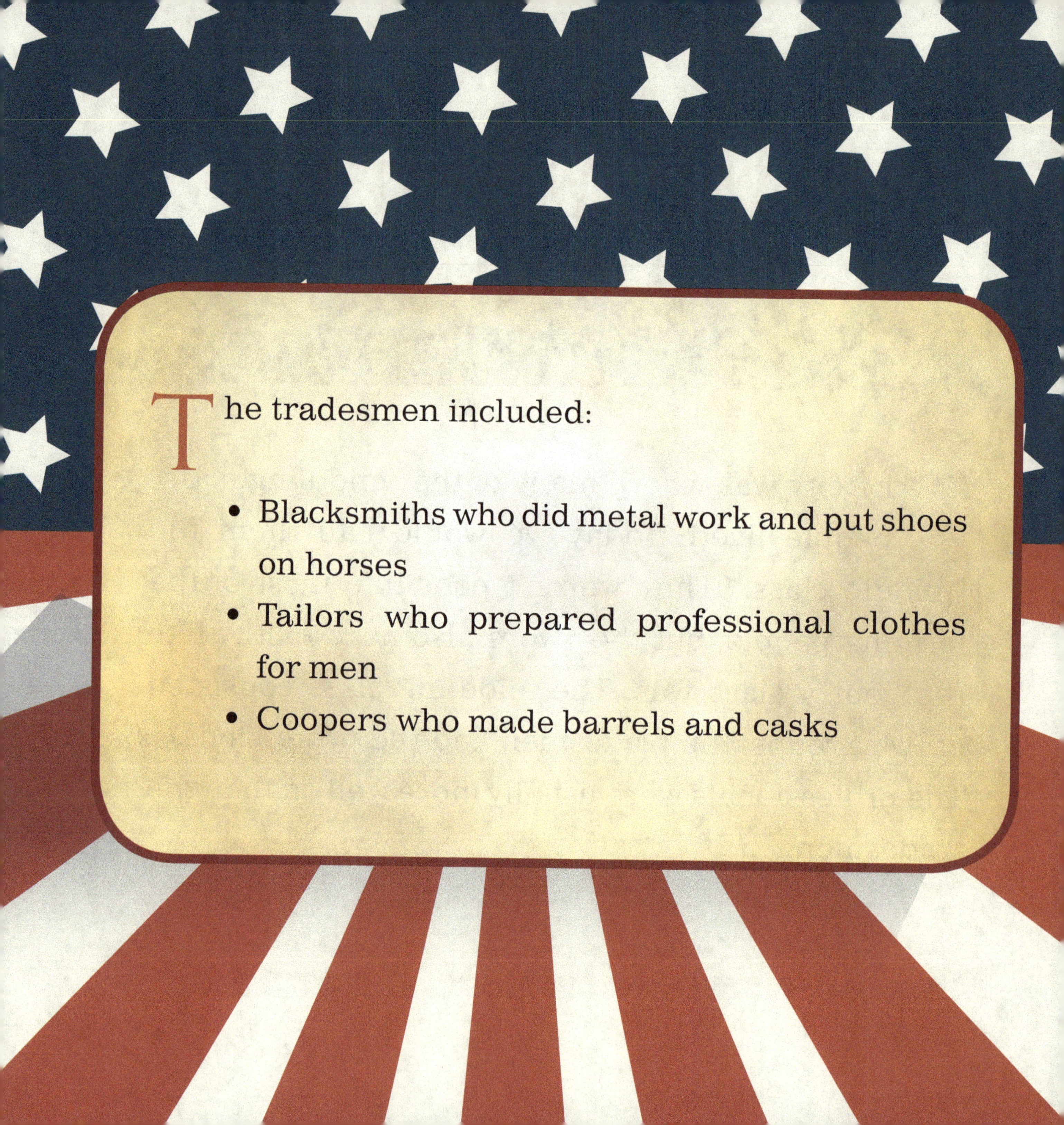

T he tradesmen included:

- Blacksmiths who did metal work and put shoes on horses
- Tailors who prepared professional clothes for men
- Coopers who made barrels and casks

BLACKSMITH

The professionals included:

- Merchants who owned the stores
- Lawyers who handled legal matters for the gentry
- Doctors who healed the sick

Although the tradesmen and professionals were better off than those who farmed, they still were hard workers and worked during all daylight hours.

SHOEMAKER

WHAT DID TRADESMEN DO?

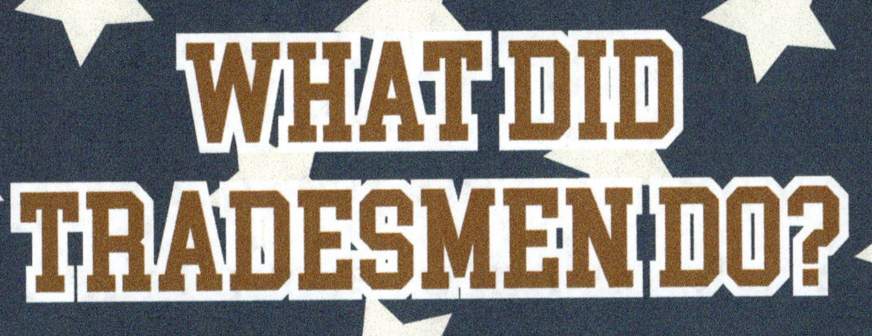

Tradesmen had very specific skills. In addition to blacksmiths, coopers, and tailors, there were wheelwrights who created and repaired wooden wheels, and shoemakers who hand crafted shoes and boots for men, women, and children.

Young boys who were the sons of tradesmen became apprentices around the age of six. They then spent the next seven or eight years learning all the details of their trade. After they finished their time as apprentices, they graduated to journeymen status. At that point, they still worked for a mentor, but earned wages.

It wasn't unusual for tradesmen to work 16 hours every day except Sunday. It wasn't easy making a living as tradesmen, however they earned enough wages to provide a good life for their families.

A YOUNG BOY SELLING VEGETABLES

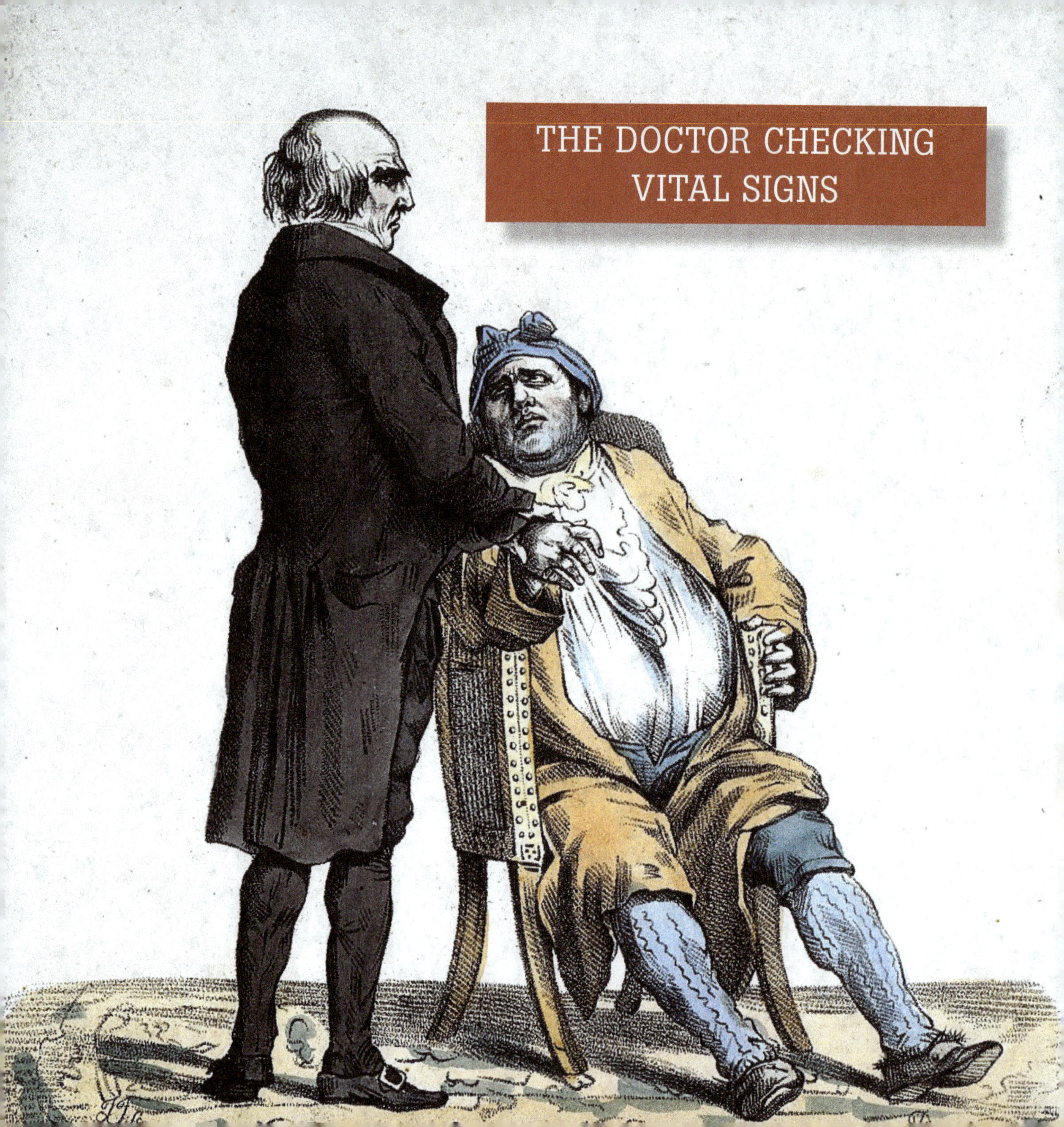

THE DOCTOR CHECKING
VITAL SIGNS

WHAT DID PROFESSIONALS DO?

Doctors and lawyers had training from a formal university in order to master their professions. Merchants sometimes had formal training from a university or trade school. In addition to understanding accounting and the business of imports and exports, most merchants had to travel to other countries. They also coordinated shipping on the docks to obtain the goods they bought and sold.

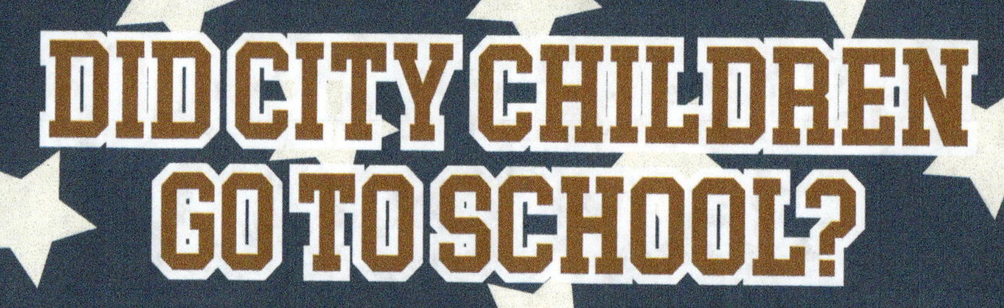

Colonial children living in cities had more of an opportunity for formal schooling than farm children had. Boys frequently attended a dame school. A dame school was a private elementary school run by a woman teacher, sometimes in her own home.

AN OLD COLONIAL RED
SCHOOLHOUSE.

S ome boys had the opportunity to go to a Latin Grammar school where in addition to the reading, writing, and arithmetic offered at the dame school, they were also taught Latin and Greek. The children of the gentry were sent to England to attend school or had private tutors who taught them at home.

BOSTON LATIN SCHOOL

THE CHURCH WAS IMPORTANT IN COLONIAL LIFE

The church was a center for community activity in colonial life. Everyone from the town was in attendance. In addition to serving as the place of worship, the town's church was also used as an important meeting place. The men of the town would meet there to discuss how to solve problems the town was facing.

WERE THERE SLAVES WORKING IN THE CITY?

Slaves worked on farms, but there were also slaves that worked in the city. They often cooked for the gentry or were their maids or personal servants. They also supported the craftsmen with skilled labor. Of course, they were expected to work hard on a continuous basis, and their masters were always around to make sure that they did.

1643
FIRST SLAVE AUCTION 1655

ST MARYS CITY HISTORIC DISTRICT
CATHOLIC CHURCH

FASCINATING FACTS ABOUT COLONIAL LIFE

The typical farmhouse had dirt floors and two rooms.

- Horses were used to work the farm, but they were also used to pull carts to travel into town. Farmers had to save half a year's earnings in order to purchase a good horse.
- Farming families attended church on Sunday.
- Despite the sweaty work, most farmers very seldom took baths. In the cities, the tavern became a place for men to meet to discuss the latest trends in politics and business.

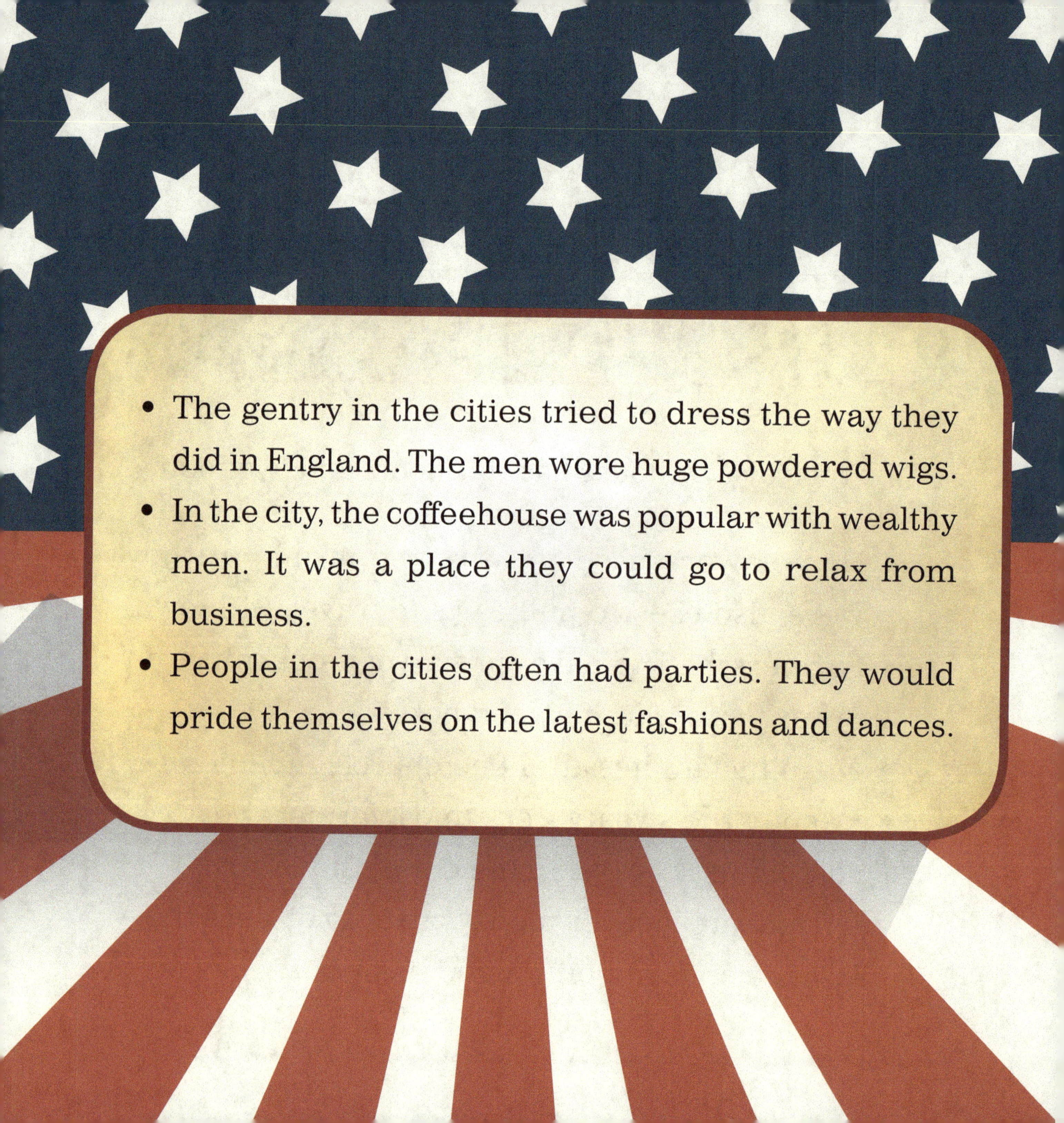

- The gentry in the cities tried to dress the way they did in England. The men wore huge powdered wigs.
- In the city, the coffeehouse was popular with wealthy men. It was a place they could go to relax from business.
- People in the cities often had parties. They would pride themselves on the latest fashions and dances.

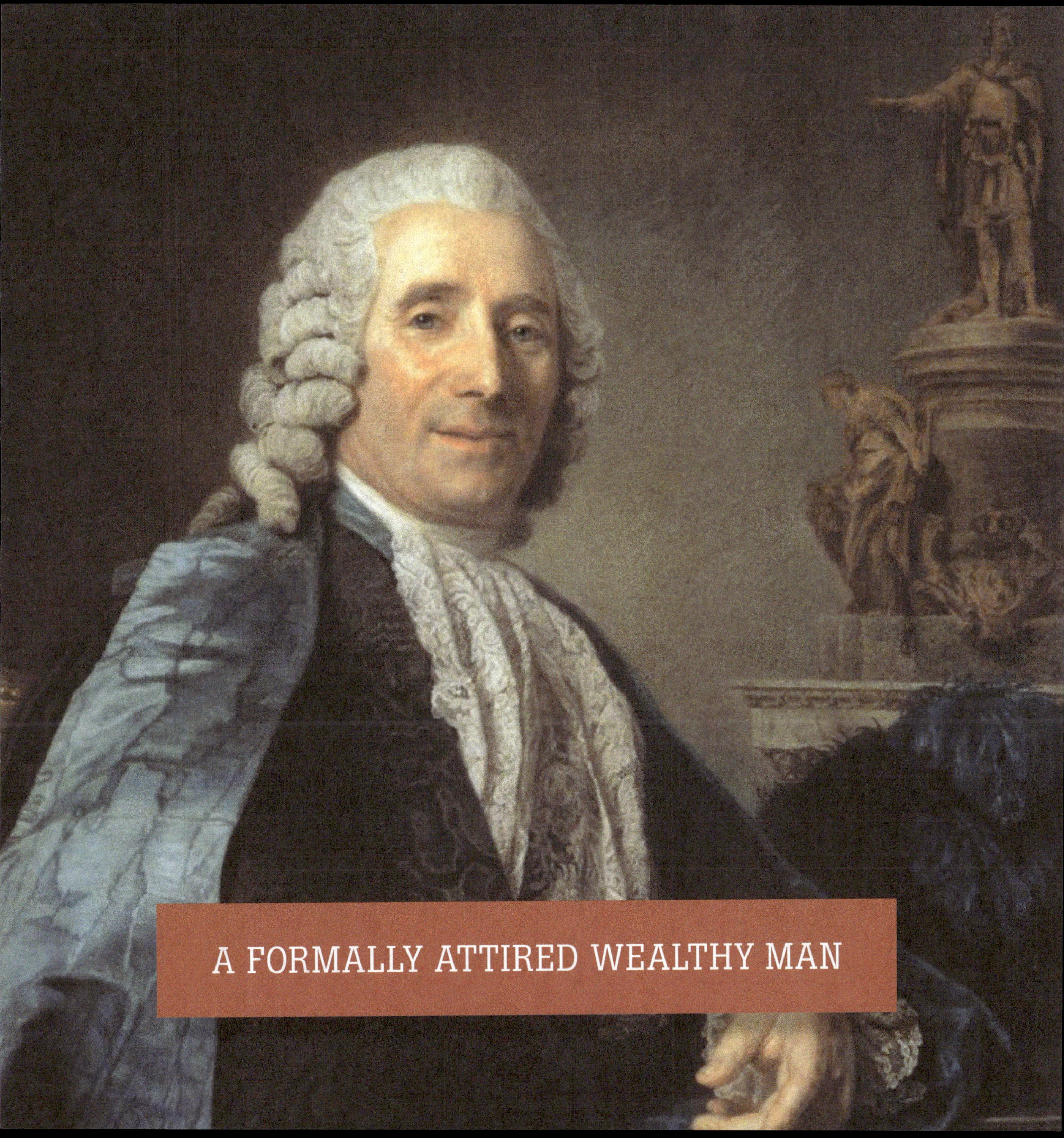
A FORMALLY ATTIRED WEALTHY MAN

SUMMARY

Life in colonial times was different depending on whether you lived in the country or in the city. Farmers and their families worked very hard during daylight hours. The men did the physical labor outdoors and their sons helped them. The women took care of the domestic chores and their daughters helped them.

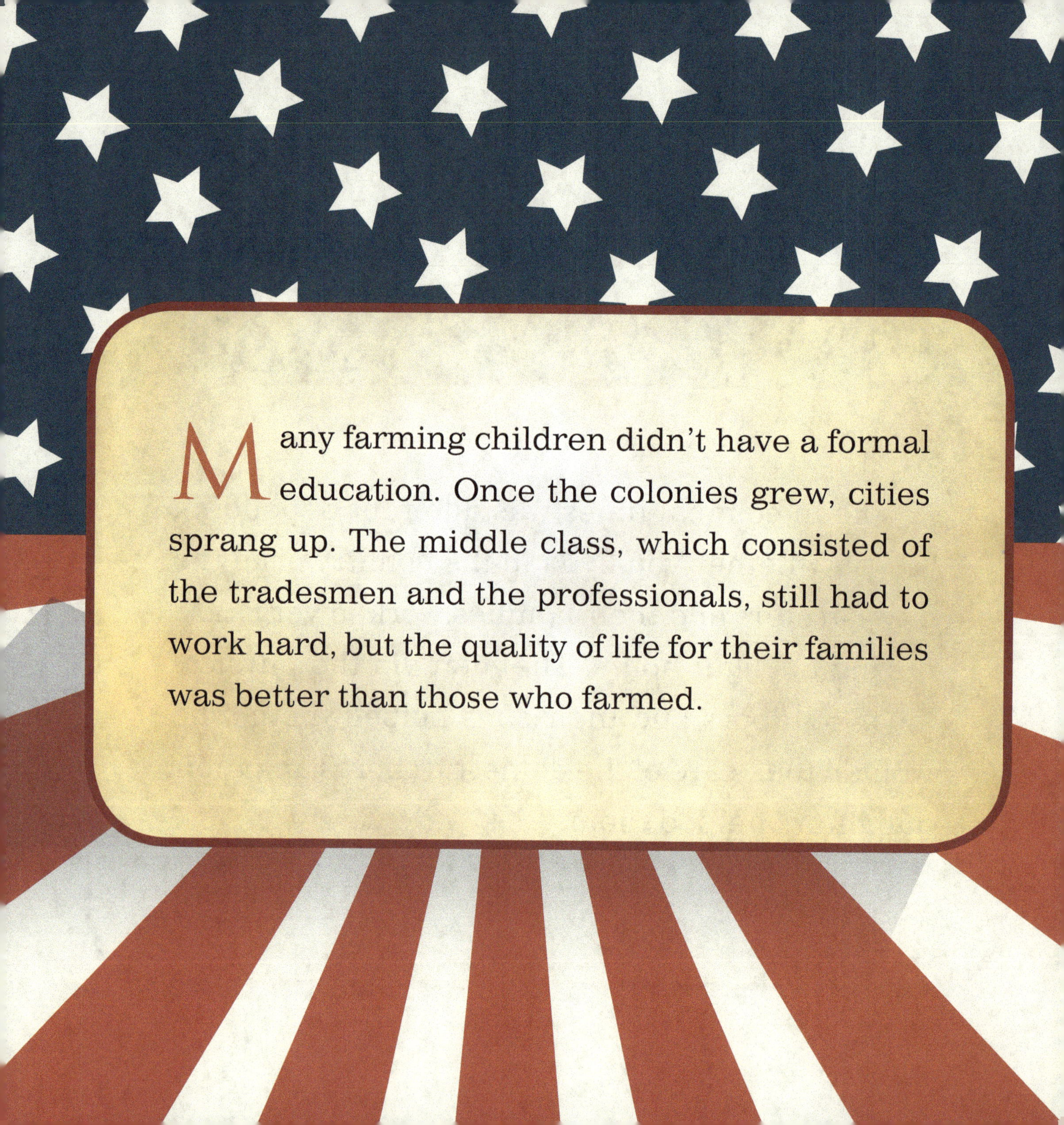

Many farming children didn't have a formal education. Once the colonies grew, cities sprang up. The middle class, which consisted of the tradesmen and the professionals, still had to work hard, but the quality of life for their families was better than those who farmed.

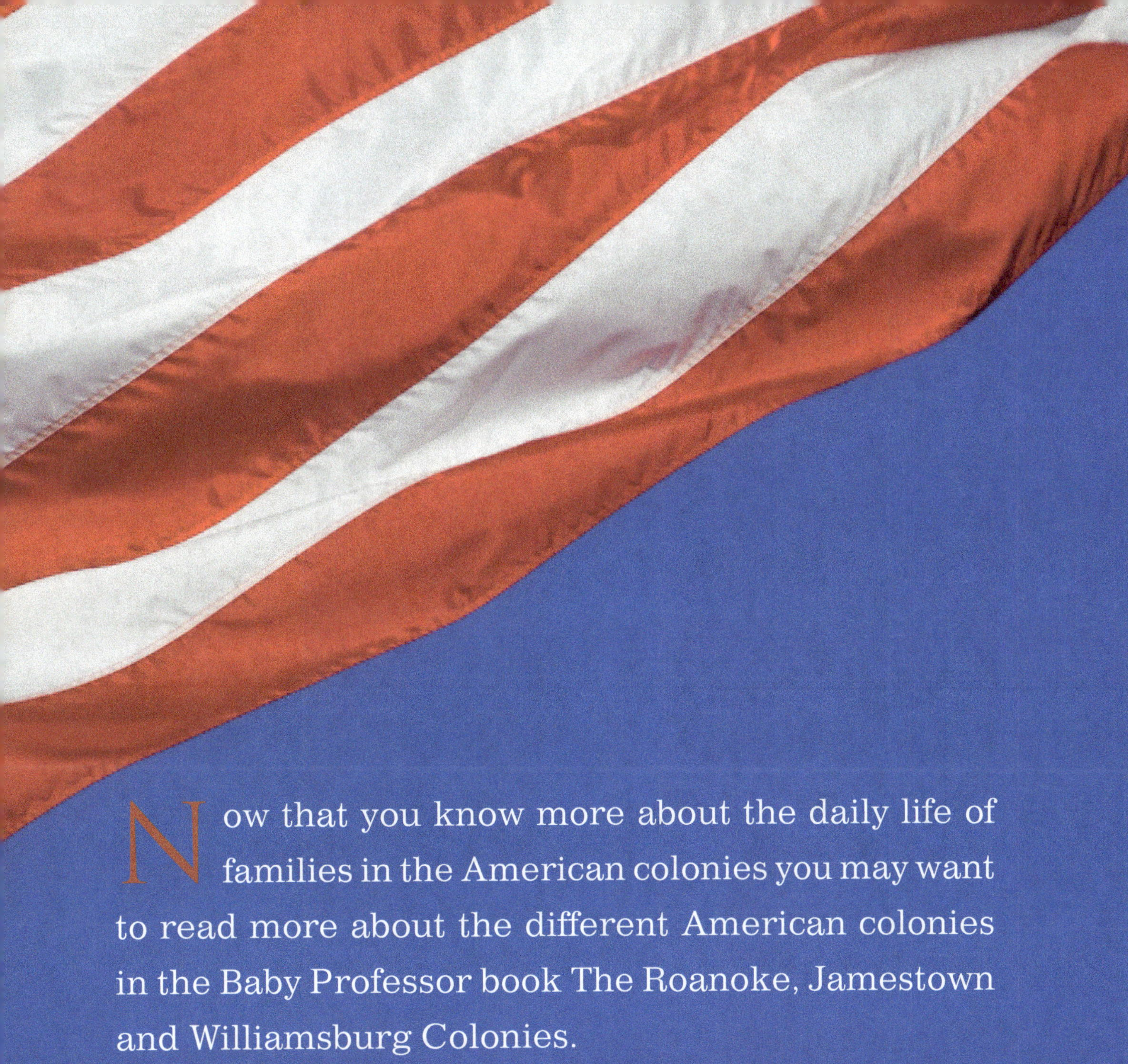

Now that you know more about the daily life of families in the American colonies you may want to read more about the different American colonies in the Baby Professor book The Roanoke, Jamestown and Williamsburg Colonies.

Visit

BABY PROFESSOR
EDUCATION KIDS

www.BabyProfessorBooks.com

to download Free Baby Professor eBooks
and view our catalog of new and exciting
Children's Books